a guide for
Compassion in
Political Power

To Tonia & Joyce!
How wonderful to be
together & share our lives —
wishing you Many Blessings!
Olivia

a guide for
Compassion in
Political Power

SYLVIA WEBER

BALBOA.
PRESS
A DIVISION OF HAY HOUSE

Balboa Press books may be ordered through booksellers or by contacting:

Balboa Press
A Division of Hay House
1663 Liberty Drive
Bloomington, IN 47403
www.balboapress.com
1-(877) 407-4847

ISBN: 978-1-4525-5337-5 (e)
ISBN: 978-1-4525-5338-2 (sc)

Printed in the United States of America
Library of Congress Control Number: 2012910346
Balboa Press rev. date: 6/18/2012

Keynote

This compelling guide to the political realities of life discusses power, control, consciousness, spirituality, and strategies to bring compassion into political power.

This guide is dedicated to all
who share my heart space

Contents

Foreword

For many years I have been encouraged by colleagues, family, friends and mentors to write and bring into the world what I teach and what I live. I agreed. For more than fifteen years I have taken courses, taken notes, written and struggled. In July 2008 I spoke with a dear friend, Sherry Carter, about my struggles. She suggested, "Let it go. When it's time Spirit will give you a sign you won't miss." Two weeks later I was at Pumpkin Hollow Retreat Center at the Therapeutic Touch (TT) Advanced Healers Invitational. Dolores Krieger, PhD, RN, co-founder of TT, gave a series of lectures, one being on compassion. During the talk we started talking about where we bring compassion into our work and lives. When I mentioned the political arena, Dee said, "Sylvia's writing a book called, "and mentioned the title. There it was and it took me by such surprise I couldn't remember the title. When I caught my breath and asked her what was the title of the book I'm writing, she said she didn't remember, it just flowed through her. Holly Majors, MSN, NP, a nurse and TT colleague, then said, "I was so impressed I wrote it down, The Compassion of Political Power." After the class, another nurse, TT colleague and a good friend, Denise Coppa, PhD, NP, showed me a note she wrote to me before Dee mentioned the book, "Sylvia, your book is about compassion and politics and here are some books you need to read." And so this guide was born.

There are many life experiences that have led me to this point and I would like to share a few that had great significance. I have always been involved in political activities and one of the strongest tests to my commitment to live a life of compassion came when I ran for the state senate in 1990, 1992 and 2006. In 1990 there were 2 of us who were running for a seat that the incumbent had held for many years. To maximize our chances of unseating him we decided to run on different party tickets, with her running in a primary. A commitment was made that if she did not win the primary, she and her supporters would work with me and my campaign. Being who this person and her supporters were and how they presented themselves in the world, I trusted them. The person did not win and a string of betrayals began, continued for 16 years and expanded. Some people, including women, who professed how important it was to elect qualified women, regardless of party (and they agreed I was qualified) were not supportive, didn't answer telephone calls or respond to letters. There was a need to address the issue, and a change in mind on their part needed to be addressed. What was called for was an honest discussion between us, one which would have taken courage, self-trust and compassion. These were important experiences for my growth. A mirror was being held up to me – was I going to allow the hurt, anger and disillusionment to encourage cynicism, isolation, to turn my back on the path I have chosen, to personalize their behavior? Or was I going to stand in my place of power, compassion, self-trust, growth and transformation? I chose the latter, which included taking responsibility for the decision I made even though a trusted friend cautioned me. The lessons learned opened new doors and provided new opportunities. After I lost the primary in 2006, I began looking at other ways I could promote the issues that are important to me. Before the primary I had received a call from the Rhode Island State Nurses Association asking if I would consider being their government relations consultant if I did not get elected. I decided to accept the position. The feedback from those I respected was very encouraging. What was especially exciting was that I had the opportunity to continue the work I was committed to, to bring compassion into politics and address policies that were for the good of the many.

There were a few experiences during my childhood that had a major role in shaping my life. I was always sensitive to my surroundings and would be the one who would intervene when peers would be aggressive or cruel towards any living being. When I was about four years old I had a recurrent dream for about one year. I would awaken in the dream state to a blue mist shaped as a woman and as she raised her robed arms a blue mist would cover me. Being young and not understanding the symbolism in the lucid dream, I would wake up screaming and crawled into bed with my parents, crying that she came for me. During my spiritual readings in my late teens and early twenties, I realized that the dream was connected to the Divine Feminine and the veil of protection. The Divine Feminine, as well as the Divine Masculine, is within us all. The Divine Feminine represents healing and protection from the place of compassion.

Another defining experience came when, during my sixth year, relatives began to arrive in the United

States from Europe as survivors of the Holocaust. Some came out of hiding, others from concentration camps. They stayed with us and other relatives until they were able to create a life here. During some evenings, when the younger ones were supposed to be sleeping, they would talk about their experiences. Being a person who never wanted to miss anything, I would pretend to be asleep. Sometimes they would only speak in Yiddish and even though I couldn't understand the words, I understood and felt the profound pain. Other times there was enough English that I experienced the human tragedy more fully. The experience was cumulative. One night I heard my cousin, Mincha, talk about what it was like to be a young, beautiful woman in a concentration camp. It is then that I made a commitment. I said to my Creator that as long as I lived, I would do something every day to make this a better world for all. Whenever I struggled to accomplish this I would remember a favorite saying of my mothers, "It's a great life if you don't weaken." I have never broken this promise.

As I reflected on these childhood experiences I realized the importance of bringing the healing energy of the Divine Feminine into the world. The Divine Feminine is the child, mother, wise woman/

crone, creation, compassion. The Divine Masculine is the boy, warrior, wise male/sage, order, provider, manifesting the material. We all have both within us and need to balance them, as well as choose which needs more expression in a particular situation. What I have found, from my personal experience, an effective way to express the healing energy of The Divine Feminine is through compassion.

Preface

Throughout history, ours, as well as other cultures, accept and tolerate many forms of violent acts toward one another – individuals, groups, nations, all forms of life and the environment. Unfortunately, our concept of violence changes with our exposure and experience so that we tolerate and minimize ever increasing acts of violence. We allow and encourage arrogance and greed, even when it destroys. In Western thought, we tend to believe in a beginning and an end instead of eternity, which allows us to be nearsighted rather than to look at our impact on all generations, present and future. We also have the false notion that we are separate from all that is around us which further allows us to hurt others and the environment. This culture and the systems within it need to be changed and healed.

George Lakoff, PhD, a professor of Cognitive Science and Linguistics at the University of California, Berkeley, in his book, "The Political Mind" makes several points which are helpful for the purposes of this guide (17). He states that we need to become increasingly aware of the cultural patterns that are a part of the structure of our brain. By doing this we can consciously change them when they do not encourage the moral foundation government is based on. Lakoff also states that government has the moral mission of protecting and empowering the people and our need to be aware of and not allow policies and directions that make government unaccountable. He uses deregulation and privatization as examples. He stresses the importance of empathy with the responsibility and strength to act on it and the current neuroscience understanding that our brains have specific centers for empathy, cooperation, and connection.

In all political arenas there are many personal agendas. This is not always bad. I have found that most people want to feel an inner sense of goodness. People in elected positions need to answer to their constituents, their contributors, their political parties, their political colleagues, etc. Lobbyists and those who pay them have an important role in the political arena when their position is not abused. They, like politicians, need to maintain a broader perspective on the impact on others and the environment we live in: what is in the highest good of the many, not the few.

James O'Dea, past president of the Institute of Noetic Science said that we created a world of simulated reality with technology (25). He said that it's now time to return to a true reality that's inclusive, because, as we know, when one suffers all suffer, when one's liberty and equality is taken away, everyone's liberty is threatened and diminished.

The purpose of this guide is to bring together many known and new ideas and information to create a way of bringing a shift, through compassion, in all of our political arenas. As Dolores Krieger, PhD, RN, stated at a conference "where we not only think deeply, we also care deeply." The guide will discuss power and control, compassion, consciousness, the spiritual dimension and strategies to create change. The information in this guide applies to all politics in life — family, friends, work - with the primary focus on government politics. Since some of the material came from discussions among family, friends, conferences, and/or colleagues, there may not always be citations and bibliography references. I apologize for these omissions.

To some, this guide may seem idealistic, naïve, ridiculous or ignorant. It depends upon your perspective. I choose to act from the concept of innocence – the ability to approach and see each situation with "new eyes" while taking into account lessons previously learned, to believe in the ability of people to change and transform, to see the good that can be and to act as if it is here now. We are as limited as our mind and spirit are. This guide and its strategies may not be a fit for you. Please, do not immediately dismiss it, without thought and/or exploration. You may find that this experience is like a mirror is being held up to you for your own growth and transformation. This may be an opportunity for change.

I would like to end the preface with a metaphor that is an underlying principle of the guide – that of the brook. The brook is always changing and its path is not always smooth. It comes to rocks and other obstacles to eventually find a way around or over the obstacle, and it keeps on flowing. We need to find a way around the obstacles and keep on flowing towards a government and society that is based on compassion for the good of the many and where the power is returned to the people.

Acknowledgements

What is written in this guide has come from many sources: conferences, workshops, readings, sharing with others, my education and work as a nurse, and my own life experiences. There are many who have supported me along my path and the writing of this book. Everyone who has entered my life at any time, regardless of how their impact was experienced or viewed at the time, has contributed to my growth and transformation. Thank you. I would like to acknowledge those who have had a direct influence on the guide and thank them for their valuable input and feedback:

Denise Coppa, Evy Cugelman, Maureen Eagan, Barbara Fuyat, Dolores Krieger, Robert Hitt, Zite Hutton, Joel Mc Crumb, Ruth Mc Intosh, Nancy Rozendal, David Shields, Deb Shields, Fran Teall, Carol Turton, and Elaine Wilk.

I would also like to thank:

- My deceased parents, Ida and Harry Weber, who were born in Russia and brought with them a strong appreciation for democracy, human rights and our responsibility as citizens.

- My eldest brother, Gerald Weber, who I would watch as he wrote letters to legislators, became disillusioned when he received the same response regardless of his position and found other ways of being involved and making a difference. I would also like to thank him for asking the questions that helped keep me on track in life and in writing this guide.

- The American Nurses Association and The American Nurses Association – Political Action Committee.

- The Rhode Island State Nurses Association and its executive director, Donna Policastro, RNP for the learning opportunities given to me as their Government Relations Consultant.

- The elected officials, their staff and the lobbyists who encouraged me and allowed me to learn from them.

- Therapeutic Touch International Association, Pumpkin Hollow Retreat Center and The Institute of Noetic Science for giving me the opportunity to test my ideas by presenting talks and giving workshops on compassion and politics

Compassion

POWER AND CONTROL:

I have met the rare person who does not want to have a sense of power and control over their lives. The majority of us do and the important factor is the type of power and the type of control we exercise. For the purpose of this guide power will be viewed as the ability or capacity to perform, to get something done. According to Elizabeth Barrett, RN, PhD, a professor at Hunter College School of Nursing, power is the capacity to participate knowingly in change (2). She also speaks of the four inseparable dimensions of power:

Awareness – of what you're doing and what
Choices – are available with
Freedom – to act intentionally with the will to have
Involvement - in creating change.

This requires the qualities and the means to carry it out. Control will be viewed as having the authority, ability, dominance to manage and direct personal and/or social activities.

Power struggles and power over others are destructive forces, a game that no one wins. If the purpose is to protect one's turf, then the action is out of fear. Fear takes away our power. When we use power through our connections, then we're dependent on others. Power through connections can be taken away. The same is true in the insider (part of the "good ole boy/girl" network) vs. outsider dynamic. The actions in this type of dynamic also encourages us to act out of fear that we may lose something. They encourage an adversarial competition and excludes the input and gifts from others and the "outsiders" which diminishes the positive impact. The dynamics that foster fear, exclusion, adversarial positions, etc. encourage us to struggle with the same issues year after year, decade after decade, the "fighting the same battle" syndrome. Personal power and control, if other and not self directed, is limited and can weaken us or a situation since the only true power and control we have is over our own actions, how we choose to respond, and how we allow life's circumstance to impact us. Is the power and control we seek for us, for others to share? Power and control over encourages us to look over our shoulder and feel owned. Is there a score card, "Look what I did for you, you owe me," or, "I'll do this for you only if you support what I want"? This position sets up the pound of flesh syndrome, and has an adversarial component. All involved want to make sure the score is kept even from their perspective. Another misuse of power is how we intimidate others to prevent them from speaking out against injustices, wrong practices, etc., to prevent "Whistle Blowing." We attempt to silence whistle blowers through threats, retribution, lies about them, overstating their behavior, publicly diminishing them, etc. If we are to use power and control for the common good, the good of the many, then we need to not act out of ego and the power of the physical form. It needs to be "us", not "me".

People involved in the political arena deal with power and control to be able to influence outcomes. When this is not balanced with an attitude of togetherness for the good of the many, with compassion, again, we are dealing with power and control over and the benefit for the few. This has been our primary mode of action and look where it has brought us — homelessness, people starving, rampant disease, bankruptcy, a dying environment, annihilation, etc.

Are we proud of this world we created and leaving for our children and grandchildren? When we join together without judgment, without personal (for me only) goals, with compassion, we are much more than the number of people present. This compassionate attitude allows us to access a greater power that is unlimited, a universal power, rather than personal power, which is limited.

When an action creates a feeling of inner fulfillment and joy it has its own power. This power not only comes from within us, it is also connected to All.

COMPASSION:

According to the dictionary, compassion is sympathy, pity, sorrow with the urge to help (42). For me this is a limited definition. Dr. Krieger, at a workshop, stated that compassion can be passive, we see and feel bad, and/or active, we do something about it. . Compassion is more than sympathy, pity and empathy. Lakoff states that empathy is an intuiting experience of the emotional states of another (17). He also states that research shows us that we are born with the capacity for empathy, a neural mechanism that tells you that you will feel better if you help. He also uses a phrase that for over 35 years I have called the platinum rule – do unto others as THEY would have you do unto them. To me, compassion is more global, more encompassing. It includes the physical, mental/emotional and spiritual planes. Both empathy and compassion are morally powerful and encourages a connection with all of life and our physical world. They're an invitation to others to feel better. Sympathy and pity can encourage enabling. Enabling allows others to not be accountable for their behavior, facilitates dependency and increases behaviors that keep them in the same situation, behavior that may not in their highest good. An example of enabling is how the economic bailout of 2008 and 2009 was created and utilized. In many instances the bailout encouraged the continuation of behavior that created the situation. Compassion encourages hope, change that encourages greater harmony. Compassion is centered in the heart and includes the word "passion". We feel it throughout us with great intensity. It transcends our own personal interest and therefore our egos are not involved. It is the heart connected to our place of all knowing (about 2–3 inches around and behind the navel) that helps to give us the ability to create. Compassion requires responsibility and strength, a willingness to be vulnerable and have no hidden agendas. This does not mean we will not experience our humanness and human emotions, such as fear, anger, pain, etc. How these emotions impact our life, how we deal with them changes. We do not allow them to determine who we are and dictate our life and actions. Compassion tends to dispel our fear when it is not related to a truly life threatening situation. It helps us to peel away the layers of who we are that are no longer useful, no longer fit, to show compassion for ourselves and to nurture.

Even though our personal interests are considered, compassion encourages us to transcend them when needed. When we lose touch with the compassionate, natural part of us, we tend to become abusive to others and the environment. Compassion encourages self confidence, self assuredness, and a willingness to educate rather than the adversarial convincing. Compassion lacks a judgmental attitude. It is the passion, the fire that feeds inspiration. It facilitates a sense of humor about ourselves, our lives and some of the absurd situations we get involved in, the ability to laugh with and not at, ourselves. Compassion also encourages us to create, what I call, compassionate distance. This is the ability to feel compassion and yet, create the boundaries and understanding that enables us to not get caught up in others chaos and drama or to take responsibility for their actions.

Gregg Braden, a former computer systems designer and computer geologist, states that heart energy is 100 times stronger electrically and 5,000 times stronger magnetically than brain energy (15). Feelings of compassion set into motion changes in the environment and the world around us. Compassions energetic vibration dissolves unnecessary boundaries, cleanses the toxicity that interferes with cooperation, and encourages harmony. It also helps us eliminate our own tendencies to interfere with and control the process.

An interesting example of this is a strategy I used when I was teaching organizational behavior at Johnson and Wales University in Rhode Island. On the first day of class I would write on the board for the students to write down their impression of the instructor, me. I would sit at the desk, reading a book, expressionless. Every other student was sent compassion as they entered the room, all the while maintaining my expressionless position. Later in the semester, when we discussed interpersonal relations, I had the students take out and share the notes they made about their first impression of me. There was much laughter. Some of the comments made by those who were sent compassion were warm, caring, smiled at them, said hello, and inviting. The other students commented on how hard, cold, and indifferent I looked. Some even said I glared at them. I used this exercise as a way to demonstrate the valuable role of compassion in the work environment and work politics.

Compassion is a way to develop practices that promote the common good and still preserve individual freedom. Compassion helps us discover the best in ourselves and others. It also helps us to see beyond the moment to the possible consequences and the actions we need to take to minimize the negative consequences. As Krieger again state during a workshop, "compassion is a mindful activation of our inner/higher self, it increases our intuitive knowing, and gives us an opportunity to take an evolutionary leap beyond our heritages."

Compassion is pure giving. It taps our innate goodness. The ego is not involved. Even though it's nice to be remembered for what we do and to be recognized, in the larger picture, in the scheme of things, recognition is not relevant and not a priority. I remember a major league pitcher, while I was growing up, who said he'd remind himself when he was in a tight spot, "In the year 2000 will anyone remember if I pitched a ball or a strike?" Unfortunately, those of us Brooklyn

Dodger fans remember what Ralph Branca pitched when we lost the World Series to the Yankees.

When we give from the heart there are no expectations, no hidden agendas, no score card and no markers to call in. It helps us to recognize when unfair and discriminatory treatment is occurring and encourages us to action to correct it. And when we model the behavior of compassion we have several additional impacts. Bandura, a social learning theorist, in Social Learning Theory, claims that observational learning, learning by watching is more powerful than learning by reinforcement and that repeated modeling reinforces the behavior(1). We are also inviting others to be in their compassionate state of being. We hold up a mirror to ourselves and others whether we come from a self-serving place or one of compassion. If being compassionate hurts you and your health, then it has gone beyond compassion and the ego, being self serving, is probably involved. For example, when I was in a private counseling practice I worked with many people in this position. They were there for everyone in their lives, giving and caring for, to the point where they were "sacrificing" their lives. They were tired, at times had difficulty focusing, became ill, etc. For some it was to the point of martyrdom. As they explored the dynamics, they realized that there were underlying motives. It may have been wanting to be needed, recognized, appreciated, feelings that they didn't deserve to do for themselves or to have others do for them, feeling totally responsible for someone, etc. When they understood the behaviors and the motivation , they were able to continue being there for others and were able to set the boundaries that were helpful for all involved.

The focus for change and healing lies in the heart. It is in harmony with our own and the Universes' nature, which is love. We do not need to learn how to be in a place of compassion or how to send compassion to others or a situation. We already know how and do this during times of tragedies and disasters, and joyful times. What we need to learn is how to focus on compassion more frequently and to open up to who we really are. It is a personal choice. And the more we call upon our innate nature the more it becomes a consistent part of our being.

CONSCIOUSNESS

The dictionary states that consciousness is being aware, aware of the totality of one's thoughts, feelings, and impressions, knowing what one is doing and why (42). We also talk about the unconscious, not being aware and yet being influenced by it, mindless, not realized or known or intended. Sometimes people use the concept of UNCONSCIOUS to justify their behavior and not take responsibility for their actions. I prefer to view consciousness as having many levels, including a cellular consciousness. Some levels are more available than others and yet are there for us to bring into our full awareness, explore, and use for our growth and transformation. Consciousness is not only our individual responsibility, it's the responsibility of our political systems and those in it to bring their actions and models into greater awareness, greater transparency. A nurse colleague and friend, Katherine Rosa PhD, RN, stated at a Therapeutic Touch meeting that people are able to move through the development of consciousness within a supportive environment rather than in the world of today. We need to develop that supportive environment if we want to create changes that encourage peace and harmony. James O'Dea states that "consciousness can be limited and divisive or can lead to a new humanity, the capacity to heal, to forgive, to deepen the bonds of friendship and love and to become an integrated whole/oneness" (25). In The Political Mind, Lakoff states, "a new consciousness demands that we cultivate empathy, self-reflection, a sense of connectedness and a full life based on them" (17).

We know when we're fully conscious by our mood, intuition, and how we feel in synchronicity, in harmony with ourselves and the world around us. By being in the present moment, we become more fully aware and more conscious. We become aware of a moral and spiritual knowing. The highest consciousness is not one of possession, it's one of being. Compassion helps us connect the various levels of consciousness and creates a state of radical knowing.

SPIRITUAL DIMENSION

For me the spiritual dimension not only includes our relationship with and within the universe, it's also our sense of purpose, direction and why we believe we are here. It's our feelings of connectedness with ourselves, with others and all of life. There are many ways people express their spirituality, organized religion being one. Regardless of how we choose to live as spiritual beings, it doesn't preclude free will.

I have found the following series of questions, when answered, can facilitate an understanding of one's spirituality and spiritual path:

- What memories do you want to create? Some people may not care if they're remembered. The reality is that we are remembered, so therefore, what would you like to be remembered for?

- What would you like your epitaph to say? This is the statement you would like your life to make. Mine is: "Here lay Sylvia under the only rock she could not turn over."

- If you had 24 hours to live, how would you spend it? This helps us to understand some of our priorities and/or our regrets, what we wished we did, and what's important to us.

- If you can dream any dream, no restrictions, what would be your dream for yourself, those who share your heart space, the country you live in, and the planet? Once you answer this, look for the themes and how, or if, you have integrated this into your life.

- After physical death, how do you believe you are carried on? This sense of immortality helps us to understand where we put our energy, what we emphasize in our lives.

- Do your beliefs and how you define yourself encourage or interfere with your being in touch with your spirituality? This helps to determine areas in our lives that need to be addressed or reinforced.

When we have a clear sense of our spiritual path, our sense of purpose, and are true to it, our possibilities are limitless. We understand that when one door closes, another opens. We understand that the opportunities are not better or worse, they are different. We understand that we are more comfortable with the concept of surrender as not giving up but rather a turning over from the physical plane to the spiritual plane while still doing what's in our control on the physical plane. We understand that the act of surrender is letting go of our attachment to the outcome. It is true that we may not get what we want and we understand that we are starting a process of change and of transformation. At a conference, a participant stated that Percy Bysshe Shelly reminds us that, "Nothing in the world is single, all things by law divine in one spirit meet and mingle".

Compassion helps us to recognize the divine, the spiritual nature in others, even if it's different from our own. Compassion facilitates our and others ability to feel joy, which is a spiritual experience. Because it is a spiritual experience we not only think globally, we act joyfully.

Compassion encourages the path of the Spiritual Warrior. The Spiritual Warrior is one who will do what he/she can to create harmony and peace, and a solution that is in the highest good of the many (18), (27). All possible strategies are explored and when appropriate implemented. When this fails the warrior position is taken and war considered, regardless of its price to the warrior. The Spiritual Warrior is also known as the Impeccable Warrior (18), (27). Compassion encourages the path of the Spiritual Warrior, a position that takes courage and self trust.

The Kabbalah states that when we are in a state of compassion we are able to silence our ego and allow Spirit to talk through us to elevate our soul and all existence, to understand and walk comfortably in the many worlds we live in (4). The Kabbalist, Baal Shem Tov, once said that there is no room for Creator in a person who is filled with themselves (5).

What is important is that at the end of the day you can look yourself in the mirror and say that you lived the day true to your values, what you claim you stand for, that you lived according to your spiritual path, without harm to others and the environment, and that if you crossed over to spirit world today, you have no regrets. And if not, we have more opportunities to learn, grow and transform to our next level.

Putting It Together

As we know and experience, we all have many simultaneous world views. In some areas of our lives we can be rigid, conservative, liberal, progressive or radical and we apply them differently. In some situations, we have varying, and at times, opposing views about the same subject. This does not have to create conflict. It can be viewed as the balance of opposites, co-existing views or feelings which give us additional information and then we choose which to act upon. The more options we have available to us, the greater our freedom to express our varied world views.

In "Social Learning Theory," Albert Bandura states that, through environmental inducements, cognitive supports and consequences for actions, people are able to exercise some control over their behavior(1). He also states that, "anticipated satisfactions, observed benefits, experienced functional value, perceived risks, self–evaluative criteria, social constraints, and economic barriers" are some of the determining factors for adopting behavior. Bandura talks about how social incentives are a way for people to influence each other without having to resort to physical consequences. He states that once patterns are well established, they are enacted without full conscious awareness. This is an important reason for our becoming more aware, more conscious of our motivation and behavior. Lakoff also talks about this in "The Political Mind "and adds that "it's important to remember that what reinforces our behavior changes with our own life experiences and development" (17). There is a continuous, influencing interaction between mind, body and spirit.

In Rousseau's, "Social Contract," he talks about two important fundamental ideas or values:

- The value of liberty, will, not force is the basis of government.

- The value of justice, right, not might, is the basis of all political society and of every system.

He believes that "only the general will can direct the powers of the State," and that these powers were instituted for the good of all (33).

We will always have conflicting concepts and there will always be some struggles about our moral and political ideas. It is the balance of opposites. You cannot have one without the other, also known as the yin/yang. We tend to reinforce what we value most and it's important to understand our beliefs and values, our interest in why we do what we do. We need to look for the best fit, not always the perfect one. When we're looking at political decisions, we need to look at the decision that creates the greatest good for the greatest number. **We often only look at the outcomes to determine our success and negate the importance of the process.**

Lakoff states that language, being an instrument of creativity and power, has a moral force that can be used to change our thinking, our minds (17). A campaign that promotes a change in policy, that is based on honesty, fact and compassion and integrates the use of language, ideas and images repeatedly, takes into account the ideas of Bandura, Lakoff, and Rousseau (1), (17), (33). It is a powerful tool for creating change for the good of the many.

Unfortunately, many of these campaigns start too late. Some campaigns are based on promoting fear and adversity, pitting constituent populations against one another, misrepresenting the facts and consequences. These campaigns are clearly based on ego and self-interest, they ignore the innate nature of compassion and cooperation. They work against our nature and are not in the highest good of self and the many. An example of this is health care reform that was attempted in the mid-70's, by the Clinton administration and, most recently, by the Obama administration. It has been clear that we needed to reform our health care system. If not, health care will become more expensive, less accessible, less efficient, and in some arenas, bankrupt. Yet, adversarial fear based misinterpretation was the order of the day. This behavior was made to seem honorable by professing to protect people who were less able to protect themselves and championing the less fortunate. Instead of looking at the collective survival, special interests pitted people against one another and curtailed individual choice. In my opinion, to continue to use a system that is broken and not working as is needed, is destructive! We know from our own experience that when a pattern, a behavior isn't working and is harmful, we need to change it or create a new one.

There are many examples of how our political system is misused. Let's look at how the bailout didn't accomplish what it was intended to. We give breaks and money to the wealthy and the oil industry that can be better utilized for promoting economic growth. One that I see on a daily basis is related to our infrastructure: our streets, roads, highways and bridges. Rhode Island, where I live, is rated in the middle of the nation for money spent on this infrastructure. Yet, I continue to see the danger to pedestrians and drivers because of the lack of safe roads and bridges, adequate street lighting, visible pedestrian crosswalks, and traffic lights. There are many areas in R.I. where a pedestrian has to walk over a mile to find a crosswalk to "safely" cross a busy street. I've had many experiences where I had difficulty crossing in a crosswalk. One time I waited over 5 minutes and one driver thought it was so great that he laughed and waved to me as he passed. However, instead of the federal government giving grants to states and create jobs to improve their infrastructure, since 1996 over $5 billion has been allocated and spent on an airborne laser that the Pentagon told Congress was not a workable concept. I remember receiving an e-mail when our economy took a downturn. It suggested that if we took all the money we have allocated in the bail out, tax breaks and subsidies for industries that have huge profits and distributed it evenly among those individuals who were 21 years of age and older, we would jump start our economy. I also agree with Walsch who states in his books "Conversations With God" that we have enough resources on this planet for everyone to have adequate shelter, food, and clothing. No one should have to live in poverty (39), (40), (41). We have enough to address every ones' needs. What gets in the way is abuse of power and greed.

There are additional examples how we protect industries and companies from being accountable. Look how long it takes us to pass standards, laws, rules and regulations that protect our environment and improve our health. Why do countries who have higher standards of product protection than the United States manage to produce and import products that meet their standards even when they come from the United States and other countries that have lower standards? Why are we not looking at the role of genetically modified seeds and fertilizers when there's an e-coli outbreak? Have we forgotten that e-coli is sometimes used to genetically modify seeds and fertilizer? And when a farm refuses to use these products, often times the winds bring them to their land. A good friend of mine, Ruth Mc Intosh, comes from Ohio and grew up on a farm. Her father and uncles refused to use genetically altered products. After her father's death, Monsanto again approached her uncles, one uncle agreed. About a year later, 4 men in suits trespassed onto the uncle's property who refused and took samples of plants and soil. Some were genetically altered, from the wind infusing his property from other farms who used these products. He subsequently has been sued for illegally getting their products and will probably lose everything. About 30 countries have agreed to ban or severely restrict genetically modified crops – including Japan, Australia, and the entire European Union. I find it interesting that some of our Secretaries of Agriculture or people in the FDA have come from Monsanto or when they leave, go to work for Monsanto who produces about 90% of the genetically modified seeds.

Laws need to be passed and enforced, and programs created that apply equally to all people, including those who create them. There cannot be a double standard if we want our people and environment to survive. We need to evaluate how we are allowing industry to pollute our environment and increase health risks and health costs. I believe that if we took half the money we spend on researching disease and invested it in cleaning the environment we would have less illness and save enough health care costs that it would be more than cost effective.

WHAT WE BRING TO THE TABLE

We bring our experiences, values, beliefs and personal characteristics to any situation and they influence how we behave and the outcome. Our view of ourselves and the world around us, and how we evaluate ourselves and our impact is also based on this. For example, will we behave differently if we value the actual or perceived reactions of others more than our own decisions and behavior? We need to consciously examine our thoughts and behavior. By doing this we will be confronted with how our behavior impacts our life, when and how we get off course, and how our cultural and family traditions impact our decisions. We need to ask if our thoughts and behaviors still fit for who we are today and do they still fit our highest good and that of the world. At times, it means stepping out of the comfort zone of our current realities.

Do you take yourself too seriously?

Then lighten up. There's a difference in taking our responsibilities seriously or ourselves' seriously. Learn how to laugh with yourself and the absurd situations we get ourselves into. I remember a card I sent to an extremely intense friend of mine in the 60's. On the cover were pictures of angels flying, with the question, "Do you know why angels fly?" When you opened it, the card said, "Because they take themselves lightly." This also reminds me of what Ann B. Ross wrote in, "Miss. Julia Speaks Her Mind" (32). Miss Julia said, "Take responsibility seriously. Don't stop having dreams, hopes. Be passionate about your life's purpose. Surround yourself with people who enhance your life and challenge your transformation. Don't grow up or lose the joy of the "aha's", adventure. Take yourself and life lightly and with a sense of humor."

Are you the type of person who tries at everything and often doesn't succeed?

Then stop trying and just do. The word try has a built in failure clause. We try at something because we have an underlying feeling, or fear it won't work or we won't succeed. When we begin to do something we gather new and additional information which can be utilized to evaluate the effectiveness of the doing. It may not be perfect and in the act of doing you can adjust your actions and your direction. You cannot do this unless you're in motion. As Henry Ford said, "Whether you think you can or think you can't – you're right." I often share with others, when the day comes that you're perfect and do not have anything to learn, to transform, then you know that you have crossed from the physical world into Spirit world. Remember, anything worth doing, is worth doing!

Are you the type of person who personalizes others' behavior?

Do you allow others to take away your dignity, diminish your self-worth? If so, for what purpose? What does it give you permission to do or not to do? Does this give others more say over your life than you, allow them to dictate your life? Is the other person's behavior holding up a mirror you don't like looking into? When we personalize others behavior, we open a door that allows them to not be accountable for their behavior because we have taken it on. Our behavior is a reflection of who *we* are, not the other person. Everything we do shares information with others about ourselves. How we behave, treat others and how we live our lives is a statement of us. Are we representing ourselves accurately, the way we want the world to know us? Are the memories you're creating the ones you want others to remember? Do you want to be remembered for what you did, or is how you accomplished it also important?

How do your addictions impact your life?

Do you recognize and acknowledge them? We all have addictions in some way. Some are more obvious than others. Addictions like alcohol, drugs, tobacco, a behavior, a person, sex, a thought pattern, food, a life style, work, children, T.V., gambling, etc., have a wide range of intensity and impact. Recognizing the struggles in dealing with them and minimizing their negative impact helps us to let go of our judgment of others and bring compassion in its place.

Do you use gossip constructively or destructively?

Peggy Chinn, a nurse, in her book, "Peace and Power: Building Communities for the Future," discusses both aspects of gossip (8). She explains that the "gossip" was like a labor coach who assisted the mid-wife during birth. After the birth, this wise woman would bring the news to the community. If the purpose of your gossip is to demean, undermine, be hurtful to another, to manipulate, to compete and be one up, to feed a feeling of self-importance, to brag about who and what you know, then it's destructive and an act of violence. When we attach labels to others or situations, attach stereotypes, it interferes with us getting as much information as possible, in really knowing and understanding all we need to. The sharing needs to have a purpose for the common good and that purpose, along with the source of information, needs to be made clear. Talking outside of the group you're involved in for clarity and ideas can be very useful. Sharing and getting feedback from others on your part in the situation and process can add to your own growth and transformation.

Barriers

We also bring with us barriers to accomplishing our goals. They come from ourselves , others, and society. Some we recognize and choose to do or not to do something about them. Some we recognize and choose not to acknowledge them. There are those barriers we are not consciously aware of. Our attachment to an outcome can be a significant barrier. That doesn't mean we don't work towards an outcome, or not want a particular outcome. It means that when we are attached to it, "it has to end this way," we lose sight of the larger picture and get caught up with ego. In the long run, it usually drains our vitality. Another way we get attached to our ego is by "getting even" -revenge. As we often say, "Payback is a bitch." Unfortunately, we get into the "pound of flesh" syndrome. "Wait a minute, you took an ounce more than I did. I have to even it up." And so the game continues. When we talk about the importance of everything we did in the past, or talk about what we're going to do in the future, this can be a barrier as well. What's important is what we do today. When we acknowledge that everything is a process, is transient, and that this too will pass, we are better able to achieve a sense of non-attachment.

Our self image can be a barrier or can enhance our ability to bring compassion into our lives and the political arena. It's okay to admit it when we don't know something. When I think of this, I think of a discussion I had with another Tai Chi student, Steve Mello. Before class we often talk about politics and sports. One day as we were talking about politics he shared with me two statements his teacher, Father Mac Mullen, a Jesuit Priest, would say in these situations: "You have constipation of thought and diarrhea of words," and, "Don't broadcast your ignorance." Admitting when we don't know something opens the door to sharing, receiving input and exploring options. When we are ego bound we tend to have a "wanna be" persona and are likely to use people and/ or situations for our self enhancement. This creates separateness and an environment of disrespect. It also encourages a sense of loneliness, a need to fill oneself because being attached to the ego creates an alienation from one's Self. When you look in the mirror, how comfortable are you looking deep into your own soul. Who do you see? When you see traits in others that you're critical of, do you use that for reflection and self growth? Do you see something in another person and experience jealousy? I remember a lesson from my mother. Since I was 9 years old, body weight has been a challenge. When I was about 10, I came home from school and said to my mother, "I want to be able to eat anything I want and not gain weight, like Madelyn." Then my mother asked a series of question: Do you want her parents, her brother, to live in her house, etc. To each I said, "No!" and repeated my initial statement with increasing frustration and finally, with anger, said, "You are not hearing me." My mother assured me that she was and then told me I wasn't hearing her. If I wanted to eat anything I wanted and not gain weight like Madelyn, I had to change places with her. It's a package deal regardless of the trait, living situation/circumstances, etc. Since that time I have not met the person I would trade places with. I'm fully aware that this is not true for many people. For me it was one of many life changing experiences. Most of us want stability, power, wealth, comfort, respect, appreciation, to be proud of who we are. It's helpful to ask: for what purpose; what are the consequences for me, others, the world, now and in the future?

Self interest does not have to be attached to the ego. If we don't have an interest in what we do, why would we do it? The key is: are we the primary focus, major recipient of the benefit or is it for our evolution and to benefit the world as well? Would you be doing this if no one will ever know? When we're aware of our thoughts and motives it brings a greater sense of connectedness with ourselves as part of the greater whole. To strengthen our self image to work for the highest good we need to remove the "veils" that block us. In Hindu it's the veil of delusions; in Buddhism it's suffering; in Christianity it's original sin, in the Kabbalah it's the klipah. Whatever your spiritual orientation, there are human blocks that need to be transformed. As we grow in wisdom we grow in self-confidence and are more willing to show and be who we are, our essence. Because we know our own strength we are able to be vulnerable, more willing to share the essence of who we are. We believe in our ability to deal with what happens to us in life. This self assurance/self trust leads to a calm inner "knowing."

When we are more aware of who we are and what we bring to various situations in our lives, including politics, we can also have a greater understanding of the impact of the law of attraction. An ancient, and shamanic saying, "what goes around comes around", is being validated by today's science. Science tells us that when we think we create energetic thought forms that travel in the form of an arch, attracting like energy. We're also told that energy, from ourselves and the world around us, imprints us and creates responses over time. Pay attention to what you focus on. Do you tend to see the more pessimistic, "cup half empty" perspective or do you tend to see the more optimistic, "cup half full" perspective? We get what we expect. As Stein states in his book "The Art of Racing in the Rain", that which we manifest is before us – intention, ignorance, successes, failures (37). Does what you do bring a sense of joy? Do you come from a place of being rather than seeking to be? Remembering the metaphor of the brook, do you keep yourself and your life flowing, open to exploring and expanding new ways of being or have you created a dam to stop the flow? Are you feeling stuck? Can you be ruthlessly honest with yourself and then have the courage to change where needed?

We are in charge of our expectations and how we view ourselves and the world around us. We can create and encourage the changes needed in us and in situations that will bring us the outcomes that we can live with and that we want for the good of the many, which includes us. This also helps us understand the many cycles of growth we experience where we repeat old patterns. This repetition helps us to test our growth to evaluate what changes are integrated and what changes we need to continue to explore. It may be helpful to remember a statement I found in a Chinese fortune cookie, "The mightiest oak in the forest is just a little nut that held its ground."

What's natural and innate within us is cooperation, compassion, being in harmony with nature, wanting to feel good, wanting to feel joy, and wanting to create balance. The more we live and express these innate qualities the more comfortable we are in living with ourselves. After all, we're the only ones we take everywhere we go and who never leave us.

ADDITIONAL STRATEGIES

A number of strategies have already been shared in this and previous chapters that would encourage the integration of compassion in our lives and in all of politics. There are additional actions that I have found useful and will address them in this section. It's useful to experiment with as many strategies as possible, including those you're not attracted to, before you discard them. Examine what about the strategies either draws or repels you. Each will give you additional information and direction. You will also be able to adapt them to better fit who you are.

Centering and Grounding

In the practice of Therapeutic Touch, a recognized nursing modality and intervention, there are two important components that I have found very useful in my life and in politics, the acts of centering and grounding. According to Delores Krieger, PhD, centering is the process of quieting oneself so that you're in touch with your innermost nature, your deepest stillness and consciousness (20), (21). This is often accomplished by going within to a quiet place where we feel in balance, notably the right and left hemispheres of the brain. Many people state they experience this when they are in prayer or while chanting. Krieger also states that, "our attention is focused on that quiet voice within, has a sense of timelessness and implicate order" (20), (21). I have found that it is also referred to as "the place of all knowing". The more we practice this, the more it becomes integrated into our everyday life and can be sustained for longer periods of time.

This state of centeredness encourages the development of insight, intuitiveness and true knowing. Along with centering comes grounding, your ability to know your place on the earth and to feel secure in it, to feel comfortably rooted – not stuck and immovable. Some accomplish this by being aware and conscious of the steps they take. Some experience themselves having roots that move with them and keep them connected to the earth. Centering and grounding helps us not to get caught up in the drama, the chaos, and keeps us focused on the present, the issue at hand and the possible solutions.

At Pumpkin Hollow Retreat Center a colleague, Betsy Ungvarsky, shared with us a centering prayer used by her friend, Sister Gail:

Be still and know that I am All.
Be still and know that I am.
Be still and know.
Be still.
Be!

Intentionality

Intentionality is another important, integral component of Therapeutic Touch, and other healing modalities, that I have found useful in the political arena. Intention is being clear, focused and honest about what is the purpose of your action. It is the exercise of judgment and keeps us in the moment. Holding an idea still leads to the beginning of intentionality. As my Tai Chi teacher, John Conroy, states, "Where thought (intention) goes is where energy goes. Where energy goes is where action goes." Intention gives energy to our actions and it is this that results in our actions impact. You know from your personal experiences, when you have one intention and "work" at behaving as if your intention is different, those around you get mixed messages. You also know that when your intention is to deceive, create fear, self-aggrandize, feed greed, you will find the actions that will accomplish this. When we do this, the energy we put into the world around us is toxic to ourselves and others because it encourages separation and fear and is for the few and not the higher good of the many. When we use the intention that our actions come from compassion, for the good of the many, it encourages us to explore other people's thoughts and concerns, to more fully understand what is involved. It's also the energy we surround ourselves and others with, an energy that's more harmonious, peaceful and transformative.

Accurate Assessment

I occasionally wonder if some of our decision makers, regardless of the political arena, would pass a competency/capacity test for decision making which requires the ability to understand information, assess the situation and to appreciate the consequences of a decision. An accurate assessment of the situation is an important aspect of bringing compassion into politics. We need to use all of our senses to pick up cues. When we are centered and grounded, only then we can also tap into our inner knowing, our intuition, for additional cues. Why are you and others contacting the politician and/or at a hearing? Where are each of you coming from? Where are the blocks? Where is the hostility? Where is the energy of compassion needed the most? The assessment process is continual. The first time I was president of the Rhode Island State Nurses Association, in the late 1980's, the executive director and I planned a meeting of stakeholders to discuss an additional direction for the association. It meant more sharing of power, to some, a sense of giving up some of their perceived personal and positional power. We arrived at the meeting place early, feeling centered and grounded, and focused our thoughts and energy on sending compassion, a loving, non-judgmental and accepting presence into the room. As people arrived, we sent compassion to each of them. When I would have some difficulty sending compassion, I would re-center, re-ground and send the color rosy-pink, which is the color of love and compassion. During the meeting I would periodically send compassion to where it was needed. The meeting went well and much needed and useful information was shared. As people were leaving, I heard the primary adversaries sharing, "I don't know what happened. Every time I opened my mouth to throw in a road block, something cooperative came out." This does not mean I had control over them. There was an atmosphere of harmony and cooperation. What it means is that I invited them to be in greater harmony with themselves, to tap what was innate. It was their choice to accept the invitation or not.

Take the route that's cooperative first, then progress from there.

Opening the Heart

There are a number of techniques available to facilitate the opening of our heart. We already do this in many cultures. For example: in prayer we tend to hold our hands over the sternum, sometimes we gently hit our chests over the heart and sternum area, or we can place our palm over or gently rub that area of our chest. I encourage you to find one that works for you.

Build Support Systems

Develop support systems that encourage growth and transformation rather than pity and rescuing. It's okay to want to be pampered and indulged at times, just not as your primary and consistent feedback. Have people who would honestly share with you your actions and thoughts that interfere with your growth, even though it might be painful. Throughout my life I have seen people undermine their accomplishments by not re-directing themselves when needed. Is this what you want or do you want to "go out at the top of your game?" Will the people in your life confront that behavior? When it's done with caring, with compassion I call it the "velvet punch." Evaluate the place and the role played by the various people in your life. In the name of "friendship", who in your life are the true friends? Part of a strong support system is having a teacher/mentor and a student/mentee. They are important roles for our continued growth and transformation. And please remember, the purpose of mentoring is to facilitate the growth of the mentee so that they surpass you. It's important to speak your truth!

Accommodation and Negotiation

Developing and refining negotiation and accommodating skills is another strategy for bringing compassion into politics as this creates a win, win solution. With this model, we begin with what is the ideal for each of the stakeholders and work together to develop solutions all can live with and can bring back to our constituents. Fear, anger, one up-manship, gloating, etc. are not present. Compromise, which tends to be our major model, does exactly what it says, everyone gives up something and feels compromised. It's a lose, lose situation even though some stakeholders beam the winning smile. Peggy Chin discusses conflict transformation in her book,

"Peace and Power: A Model for Future Communities" (8). During the process the group addresses where there is diversity and where there is unity. They define and re-define the conflict and each person's part in the conflict and/or resolution and develop strategies that the group can utilize to transform the conflict. When the strategies do not bring resolution she discusses going beyond the usual: "Let's agree to disagree." It's important to develop strategies that encourage actions that will enable us to live with the differences without creating harm. As stated earlier, it's important to use language constructively and to be creative. When we are working on issues and/ or building coalitions, invite as many of the stake holders as is possible and stay in a place of compassion during meetings. This requires strength, courage and focus while involved in group processes for the good of the many.

The Energy of Caring/Important Questions

Lakeoff discusses caring, which is not only empathy, but also taking action with responsibility and strength (17). This also entails asking what are the policies consequences and how does it affect all that we are connected to? In many indigenous cultures, including The Iroquois Confederacy, the question asked is not only related to the present time. The question asked is: how will this impact the next 7 generations? Would we be in the position we're in now if we always asked that question? Personally, I don't think so. We'd be much better off.

Another question that would be useful to ask in the political arena is, "what and who is motivating this policy, this change?" Who or what forces are dictating this movement? Is it that the right person with the right connections has just had their life impacted significantly by a situation? When involved in lobbying I often hear how we have to change - (you can fill in the blank) and that people are abusing the system. I hear about the neighbor, relative, or acquaintance, who they know should not be receiving "these benefits." Personally, I cannot think of a system that is not abused by someone. From my own experience, I have also discovered that the number that abuse the system are far less than those who don't and who rightfully benefit from the system. Why do we allow the abusing few to dictate rather than the many who don't? Why not change the system to minimize the abuse? All systems change; we need to be clear what change we want. As my friend, Nancy Rozendal, Ph.D, PCNS, a nurse therapist, says, "Change creates growth when it's effectively managed. To create change, we need to increase the number and strength of the driving forces" (35). I add, for the good of the many.

To further encourage the integration of compassion in the political arena, I believe there are several additional practices that need to be changed. Campaigning strategies is one of them. There has been concern expressed about the lengthy campaigning and the cost. Much of the time it's not the best candidate who wins, it's the one with the most money. With our campaign finance practices we significantly limit the qualified candidate field. Attempts have been made to change that. From my perspective, it was unfortunate that the Supreme Court made a decision that encourages the potential for more abuse. This decision contradicts our value of open and transparent government. The anonymity discourages us from knowing who may be involved and "owed." Personally, I would like to have the option during primaries that state "none of the above" or "go back to the drawing board". I also believe it would be helpful if we discouraged attack and smear campaigns and promoted an attitude of respect. The candidates are not running against each other; they are running for the same seat, based on who they are, their credentials, and what they will bring. After all, if you don't believe in yourself and your credentials, why are you running? In the October 2010 issue of the AARP Bulletin, Jim Leach wrote an article, "Civility in a Fractured Society." In the article he talks about how "rancorous politics" is dividing Americans. He also commented that "Civility is not simply about manners. It doesn't mean that spirited advocacy is to be avoided. What it does require is a willingness to consider respectfully the views of others, with an understanding that we are all connected and rely on one another." Along with these changes, candidates, once elected need to address their campaign promises. If a campaign promise cannot be kept, the public has a right to know why. Is there new data, the benefits are not worth the time and energy it would require, there are more blocks than were expected? We need to continue the effort for changing campaign practices until it happens.

Along with this is the role the media plays and how they encourage these practices, as well as other destructive behavior in the name of selling newspapers. I'm not suggesting not reporting these events, I'm suggesting a better balance and placement of articles, to encourage actions of courage, cooperation and compassion and not to undermine them. When Hillary Clinton was in a primary with President Obama, I often reflected on some of the differences in reporting. My favorite example was a radio report where he received about one minute of quotes that reflected his plan followed by one quote from her, "I have earned every one of my wrinkles." Do you think a female candidate who was a centerfold for Playboy magazine would receive the same response as a male candidate who was a centerfold for Cosmopolitan? I don't think so. It's important to report all perspectives equally and honestly and to claim your biases. Bandura states that an influential source of social learning is the modeling of T.V., films and other visual media (1). We need to just look at the impact of some of the video and computer games, movies, etc. I personally do not believe that the right, "freedom of speech," was intended to be synonymous with presenting views that intentionally pit people against one another and foster hate and fear. Look how our technology has been used to abuse and destroy. All forms of media needs to be held accountable.

Our justice system also needs to be held accountable and do what the word implies, justice, equally applied, not based on race, religion, gender, age, money, or fame. For example, well known and/or rich people need to receive the same consequences for the same or similar offense as anyone else.

There are certain positions that lead to a more public life: elected officials, sports, entertainment, etc. When one chooses to enter these realms there are tradeoffs that are made. Those tradeoffs relate to one's private life, which becomes less private. Take responsibility for that decision and be aware of the tradeoffs/changes that will occur.

When communities, professions, etc. are having difficulty, we need to include in committees and task forces representation of those who will and are affected. How often do we see boards of organizations, committees, task forces, etc. making decisions without representation of those who will be impacted.

On reflecting on the various wars we have been involved in during my lifetime, I agree with the practice of some indigenous cultures, that the women have a role in declaring war, since war sacrifices our children. I often wonder how many wars we would have if the leaders who declare war, along with the people they care about, are at the beginning of the front line, followed by all government officials who agree with the war and their loved ones, followed by all those who support the war, and so on. How many wars would we have if the presidents, prime ministers, leaders, along with their loved ones took the first step onto the battle field? Some would say, "We can't do that, they're too important." I agree with a German journalist who wrote in his column after the assassination of John F. Kennedy, that when we are as horrified at the assassination of the common person, we know that we have made progress. Everyone is important and has a contribution if we encourage and honor it.

As I've stated before, being in a place of compassion and utilizing these strategies, does not mean we do not experience the human emotions of fear, anger, and wanting revenge. We need to acknowledge them, give them permission and then put them aside or at times muddle through them and not allow them to dictate our behavior. When we repeatedly model compassion we reinforce positive behavior. It takes time to create change. At first the beginning steps of change are not noticeable. Continue the process you began. Continue to open the door for yourself and others. Don't give up. When change starts to occur, continue not to give up, keep the reinforcing modeling going. There are many layers to go through to create a permanent change. For me, good examples of our stopping the momentum too soon is the Civil Rights and the Women's Movement. We did not wait for permanency and in many areas, how far have we really come?

Summary

History has many examples that show us that powerful societies who abuse their power to achieve power over without regard for the many, over time do not survive or are diminished. It's time we learn the lessons. There will always be disagreements, conflicting concepts, beliefs, and values. What's important is how we resolve them. Each individual and society has a responsibility to the global whole.

During the 60's when busing was used to promote integration, a number of my friends, with children and without, believed in this as they would preach from their homes in communities where busing was not possible. I was the only one in the group that lived in an integrated neighborhood. From a place of affection, I would refer to them as armchair activists. I encourage you to challenge yourself. These challenges do not have to be very stressful or create angst, they can be fun and joyful, a wonderful adventure. What would it take to make the transformative changes we need in this world and ourselves? A commitment to doing it! Move one step at a time and enjoy the doing. Do one thing along this path each day. When you're imagining what this world of compassion would be like, don't only live it in your mind, experience it in your entire being. See what can be in the future and live it today, using discernment. Dante, in The Divine Comedy, talks about the ability of love/compassion to save humanity (10). He states that when we abandon this path we lose hope and then live in the desire for transformation without a plan. Don't abandon the path.

This guide is not a request for a leap of faith. It is a request to allow compassion and cooperation guide and become one with your heart. There's a Native American story (author unknown), a metaphor, that is an example of what is being talked about in this guide. An old warrior is telling his grandchild about the two wolves warring inside of him. One wolf is loving, compassionate, is concerned and works for the good of the many, the good of all of life. The other is mean, destructive, and only wants for the self. When the grandchild asks which one wins, the grandfather replies, "The one I pay attention to."

Pay attention to your thoughts and actions. Which wolf is winning?

I encourage you to utilize your support systems to support change and to raise other people's consciousness. We all touch many lives and can easily, with today's technology, create global networks to achieve this. We can also become part of one that already exists. With this increase of compassionate consciousness we can reach what Keyes calls the 100th monkey principle, a shift in consciousness (19). Even a small, what may appear as an insignificant reflection and change impacts us and the world. As Gandhi stated, "Live as if you are going to die today. Learn as if you will live forever."

Writing this guide has been a wonderful journey for me, another layer of growth and transformation as I confronted old and new insecurities, ego issues – would it be good enough, will it make a difference, would I be ridiculed, etc. I frequently thought about the story of the starfish, adapted from "The Star Thrower," by Loren Eisley, (13), where a young child is walking along the beach filled with starfish, patiently returning them to the ocean. An older adult sees the child and asks, "Why are you doing this, you can't save them all. You can't possibly make a difference." The child picked up another starfish, returned it to the ocean and said, "I made a difference to that one." If this guide makes a difference in one life, I have accomplished my goal.

I would like to share a 2010 New Year's e-mail I received from the Board of Trustees of Therapeutic Touch International Association.

Peace on Earth

Let this be a year when wars might end and peace may begin

Let this be a new year where acceptance and tolerance becomes abundant

Where passion finds an anchor and laughter lifts up volumes of love.

Let this be a new year where we find hope, and dreams are fulfilled

Where blame disappears and responsibility becomes our code of honor

Let this be a new year where our collective hearts reach out on a global level to those in need.

Where what we give we receive

Let this be the year where music dances with and in our spirits.

Let this be a year that heals and empowers the soul of the earth.

Let this year be the year that begins all years

To follow in the footsteps of peace on earth and good will to every being

Everywhere!

Author Unknown

Kadeeshtay – May you walk in beauty!

Bibliography

1. Bandura, Albert. "Social Learning Theory." Prentice Hall, NJ. 1977
2. Barrett, Elizabeth. Workshop at Pumpkin Hollow Retreat Center, Craryville, NY. 2008
3. Beckwith, Michael Bernard. "Life Visioning." Sounds True. 2008
4. Berg, Rav. "The Wisdom of Kabbalah." The Kabbalah Center, LA, CA. 1999
5. Berg, Yehuda. "Out of the Darkness." The Kabbalah Center, LA, CA. 2006
6. Besant, Annie. "The Bagavad Gita." The Theosophical Publishing House, Wheaton, IL. 1978
7. Bland, Betty." From Pebble to Stepping Stone." The Theosophical Society, Quest – Winter 2009. Wheaton, IL
8. Chin, Peggy. "Peace and Power: Building Communities for the Future." NLN Press. NY, NY 1995
9. Dalai Lama. "Universe in a Single Atom." Morgan Road Books, NY, NY. 2005
10. Dante, Alighieri. "The Divine Comedy." Biblio Bozaar, 2007
11. Doidge, MD, Norman. "The Brain That Changes Itself." Penguin Books, NY, NY. 2007

12. Doreal. "The Emerald Tablets." Source Books, Inc., Nashville, TN, 1939.

13. Eiseley, Loren. " The Star Thrower." Harvest Books/ Times Books. NY, NY. 1979

14. Capra, Fritjof, "The Tao of Physics." Shambhala Publications Inc. Boston, MA. 1975

15. Global Coherence Initiative. www.glcoherence.org

16. Johnson, Spencer. "Who Moved My Cheese?" G.P. Putnam's Sons, NY, NY. 1998

17. Lakoff, George. "The Political Mind." Viking Penguin, NY, NY. 2008

18. Keetowah. Oral Teaching. 1984 – 1992

19. Keyes, Ken. "The 100th Monkey." Vision Books, Coos Bay, OR. 1982

20. Krieger, Dolores. "Accepting Your Power to Heal." Bear and Co. Sante Fe, NM. 1973

21. Krieger, Delores. "The Therapeutic Touch." Prentice Hall, Inc. Cliffs, NJ. 1979

22. Mc Clelland, D.C. "The Two Faces of Power." In Lorsch, J.W. and L.G. Barnes, ed. "Managers and Their Careers: Cases and Readings." Richard D. Irvine, Inc. Homewood. IL. 1972

23. Mc Taggart, Lynne. "The Intention Experiment." Free Press, NY, NY. 2007

24. Novick, Rabbi Leah. "On The Wings of Shekhinah: Rediscovering Judaism's Divine Feminine." Quest Books, Wheaton, IL. 2008

25. O'Dea, James. "A Vision Forward." Shift, IONS Publication, Winter 2008-2009

26. Ornish, D. "Love and Survival: The Scientific Basis for the Healing Power of Intimacy." Harper Collins, NY, NY. 1998

27. Oh Shinah. Oral Teachings. 1981 – Present

28. Roberts, Jane. "The Seth Materials." Prentice Inc. 1970.

29. Roberts, Jane. "Seth Speaks: The Eternal Validity of the Soul." Prentice, Inc. 1972

30. Roberts, Jane. "The Education of Oversoul Seven." Amber-Allen Publishing. 1973

31. Roberts, Jane. "The Nature of Personal Reality: A Seth Book" Amber-Allen Publishing. 1974

32. Ross, Ann. "Miss Julia Speaks Her Mind." Harper Collins Publishers, NY, NY. 1999

33. Rousseau, J. "Social Contract." , "Social Contract: Essays by Locke, Hume and Rousseau." Oxford University Press, London. 1953

34. Rousseau, Jean-Jacques. "Emile: On Education." Translated by Allan Bloom. Basic Books, 1979

35. Rozendal, Nancy. "Power, Politics, and Change: Unionization." Handbook of Psychiatric – Mental Health Nursing, Adams, C. and Macione, B. eds. John Wiley and Sons, NY, NY. 1983

36. Shinoda Bolen, Jean. "Goddesses in Every Woman." Harper and Row. San Francisco, CA. 1984

37. Stein, Garth. "The Art of Racing in the Rain." Collins Publishers. NY, NY. 2008

38. Tolle, Eckhart. "A New Earth: Awakening to Your Life's Purpose." Plume Penguin, NY, NY. 2005

39. Walsch, Neale Donald, "Conversations With God: Volume I." Hampton Roads Publishing Co., Inc. Charlotsville, Va. 1995

40. Walsch, Neale Donald, "Conversations With God: Volume II." Hampton Roads Publishing Co., Inc. 1997

41. Walsch, Neale Donald, "Conversations With God: Volume III." Hampton Roads Publishing Co., Inc. 1998

42. Webster's New Collegiate Dictionary. G&C. Merriam Co. Springfield, MA. 1977

43. Whitley, Richard. "The Corporate Shaman: A Business Fable." Harper Collins Publishers, Inc. NY, NY. 2002